To: Lila —

My longtime Christian friend —

May God continue to bless you

in every way!   Feb 6, 2016

Happy Birthday!

Sing Unto

the

LORD

Sing Unto

the

LORD

~ Hymn Titles in Poetry ~

Connie Campbell Bratcher

Pearl
Publications
Sharpsburg, Georgia

Published by Pearl Publications, Inc.
Sharpsburg, Georgia

Scripture quotations from the Holy Bible, King James Version
All poetry by Connie Campbell Bratcher

Cover painting by
D.D. (Dwight) Watson
Fayetteville, Georgia

Design and color illustrations by
Gabriele Ervin
San Antonio, Texas
Your Impressions Co.

ISBN 978-0-9774190-5-0

Signature Book Printing, Inc.
www.sbpbooks.com
First Printing, October, 2015
Printed in USA

Introduction

Nothing can lift our hearts in worship and praise more than singing the great hymns of the faith. They are such a vital part of our Christian heritage! Thanks to hymn writers, such as Isaac Watts, Charles Wesley, John Newton, Fanny Crosby, and many others, we have a rich storehouse of songs that link us to the earliest Christians. The singing of these hymns reinforces Bible truth in our hearts, for they are full of theology! They contain messages that not only inform, enrich, and edify our faith, but can bring conviction of sin, unite us in prayer, rejoice the heart, and draw us into a closer walk with our Lord and Savior Jesus Christ. We cannot afford to let our children and children's children miss out on the treasures found in these great old hymns of the faith.

It is my prayer that this volume of Inspirational Messages in Poetry, containing titles of some of our very favorite hymns, will lift you, bless you, and cause you to… "Sing Unto the LORD."

~ Connie Campbell Bratcher

"Sing unto the LORD,

bless his name;

shew forth his salvation

from day to day."

(Ps 96:2)

Come, Let Us Sing!

"We've a Story to Tell to the Nations,"
For "There is a Fountain," friend...
One that will give eternal salvation,
Wash away sin, heal, and mend.

Let us "Go Tell It on the Mountain,"
"Jesus Saves" from sin and shame;
"O For a Thousand Tongues to Sing"
"Glory to His Name"!

"O COME, let us sing unto the LORD: let us
make a joyful noise to the rock of our salvation."
(Ps 95:1)

1

He Keeps Me Singing

"Brethren We Have Met to Worship,"
O "Blest Be the Tie That Binds."
Come, "Let Us Break Bread Together,"
"What a Fellowship" divine!

"All That Thrills My Soul is Jesus,"
"He is So Precious to Me."
"He Keeps Me Singing" as I go…
"One Day" His face I shall see!

"I will sing unto the LORD as long as I live:
I will sing praise to my God while I have my being."
(Ps 104:33)

Face to Face

"When I Survey the Wondrous Cross,"
Where "Jesus Paid it All,"
I cry, "Holy, Holy, Holy"…
"Down on My Knees" I fall.

"Heaven Came Down," "Love Lifted Me."
Praise God for "Amazing Grace"!
"O That Will Be Glory for Me,"
When I see Him "Face to Face."

"Now we see through a glass, darkly;
but then face to face."
(1Cor 13:12a)

Power in the Blood

"Sing the Wondrous Love of Jesus,"
"O How He Loves You and Me"!
"He is Able to Deliver Thee,"
For "His Blood Still Sets Men Free."

Such "Wonderful Grace of Jesus,"
"We Have Heard the Joyful Sound."
Friend, "There is Power in the Blood"!
It can lift to "Holy Ground."

"Ye were not redeemed with corruptible things,
as silver and gold... but with the precious blood of Christ,
as of a lamb without blemish and without spot."
(1Pet 1:18a-19)

A Living Sacrifice

I'm "Saved By His Power Divine,"
"There is Sunshine in My Soul"!
"Alleluia," "I'm Free, Free, Free"...
"He Touched Me, and Made Me Whole."

"Rock of Ages," "How Great Thou Art."
"At the Cross," You paid the price...
Lord, "Take My Life and Let it Be"
For Thee "A Living Sacrifice."

"I BESEECH you therefore, brethren, by the mercies
of God, that ye present your bodies a living sacrifice, holy,
acceptable unto God, which is your reasonable service."
(Rom 12:1)

Lead Me, Lord

"Take My Life, Lead Me, Lord,"
"I Surrender All" to Thee…
Teach me, "Speak to My Heart,"
"Holy Spirit, Breathe on Me."

"I Need Thee Every Hour,"
"Abide With Me" I pray.
"Draw Me Nearer," Lord, to Thee…
"A Closer Walk," each day.

"Teach me thy way, O LORD, and lead me
in a plain path."
(Ps 27:11a)

The Blood of Jesus

"Nothing but the Blood of Jesus"
Can remove sin from the soul.
"At the Cross," our Lord receives us
And brings us into His fold.

Thank God for "The Old Rugged Cross,"
And His supreme sacrifice;
"All Hail the Power of Jesus Name,"
His precious blood paid the price.

"In whom we have redemption through his blood,
even the forgiveness of sins."
(Col 1:14)

The Anchor Holds

"I Am Bound for the Promised Land,"
A pilgrim on earth's sod;
"My Faith Has Found a Resting Place"
"Near to the Heart of God."

Such "Wonderful Peace" our Lord gives
"In the Haven of Rest."
"The Anchor Holds" and we are safe
Through every trial and test.

"Which hope we have as an anchor for the soul,
both sure and steadfast."
(Heb 6:19a)

8

The Comforter Has Come

"Praise God, From Whom All Blessings Flow,"
"The Comforter Has Come."
O "Jesus, Lover of My Soul,"
Sweet victory is won!

The promised Holy Ghost of God
Is with us as we pray;
"Love Divine, All Loves Excelling,"
He's our guide "Day By Day."

Jesus said: "I will pray the Father,
and he shall give you another Comforter,
that he may abide with you for ever."
(Jn 14:16)

He Will Set You Free!

"When We Walk With the Lord"
"In the Garden" of prayer,"
The "Spirit of the Living God"
Is always there.

O friend, "My God is Real,"
And "He Leadeth Me."
"Turn Your Eyes Upon Jesus,"
He will set you free!

"The law of the Spirit of life in Christ Jesus hath
made me free from the law of sin and death."
(Rom 8:2)

Fill My Cup

O what would we do "Without Him"?
How thirsty we would be!
"As the Deer Pants After Water,"
Lord, our souls pant for Thee.

"Come Thou Fount of Every Blessing"
Provided "At Calvary"...
"Like a River Glorious," Lord,
"Fill My Cup" eternally.

"As the hart (deer) panteth after the water brooks,
so panteth my soul after thee, O God."
(Ps 42:1)

Wherever He Leads I'll Go

"I've Got a Home in Gloryland,"
And "One Day" "I'll Fly Away"!
But "Until Then" I'll serve my King,
Rejoicing every day.

"Heavenly Sunlight" fills my soul,
Such blessings He doth bestow!
"'Tis so Sweet to Trust in Jesus,"
"Wherever He Leads I'll Go."

Jesus said: "If any man serve me,
let him follow me."
(Jn 12:26a)

How Firm a Foundation!

"On Christ the Solid Rock I Stand,"
"How Firm a Foundation"!
"He Included Me" in His plan;
Praise God for salvation!

Lord, "Standing on the Promises,"
"My Faith Looks Up to Thee."
"Leaning on the Everlasting Arms,"
I'm safe eternally!

"Other foundation can no man lay than that
is laid, which is Jesus Christ."
(1Cor 3:11)

Precious Name!

"O God, Our Help in Ages Past,"
Our hope, our victory,
"Give Me That Old Time Religion,"
"It's good enough for me"!

"I Will Sing the Wondrous Story,"
Thou art ever the same!
Jesus, Son of the Living God...
O what a "Precious Name"!

"Glory ye in his holy name: let the heart
of them rejoice that seek the LORD."
(Ps 105:3)

He Touched Me

Praise be to God, "I'm Born Again"!
There's been a change in me.
I'm now "A Child of the King,"
Serving Him eternally.

"Jesus, Name Above All Names,"
Redeemer of my soul,
"Showers of Blessing" surround me...
Since Your touch made me whole.

"As many as he touched were made
perfectly whole."
(Matt 14:36b)

15

O How He Loves You and Me!

"Are You Washed in the Blood?"
"Christ Receiveth Sinful Men."
"Softly and Tenderly" He calls...
He is our dearest Friend!

"The King of Glory," Lord of all,
Came to earth to set us free.
"There's Room at the Cross for You"...
"O How He Loves You and Me!"

Jesus said: "Greater love hath no man than this,
that a man lay down his life for his friends."
(Jn 15:13)

16

In Times Like These

"In Times Like These," we need the Lord
To anchor our drifting soul.
"The Light of the World is Jesus,"
Come to Him and be made whole.

"Jesus is Tenderly Calling,"
His Spirit is in this place.
"Whosoever Will May Come"...
He will save you by His grace.

"The Lord is not slack concerning his promise,
as some men count slackness; but is longsuffering
to us-ward, not willing that any should perish,
but that all should come to repentance."
(2Pet 3:9)

What the World Needs Now

"What the World Needs Now Is Love"...
God's love, genuine and true.
"Brighten the Corner Where You Are"
And His love will shine right through.

This "Amazing Love," so divine,
Is a fruit we are to bear;
"Seek Ye First the Kingdom of God"
And you'll have enough to share.

Jesus said: "Herein is my Father glorified, that ye bear
much fruit; so shall ye be my disciples."
(Jn 15:8)

So Send I You

"People Need the Lord," this we know,
But how shall they hear, my friend?
Who is to tell them? Who will go?
Do we hear God's voice within?

The fields are white, it's "Harvest Time,"
Yet the laborers are few;
O Christian, the Master's calling…
Hear His voice, "So Send I You."

"Then said Jesus to them again, Peace be unto you:
as my Father hath sent me, even so send I you."
(Jn 20:21)

Safe in the Shepherd's Fold

Christian, when we walk through the storm,
There's no need to ever fear;
We're "Sheltered in the Arms of God,"
And His Spirit is so near.

His timing is always perfect!
He is in complete control;
"Through It All," our Lord carries us...
We're safe in the Shepherd's fold.

"For he is our God; and we are the people of his pasture,
and the sheep of his hand."
(Ps 95:7a)

Press On

"A Mighty Fortress is Our God"...
"A Shelter in the Time of Storm."
"Blessed Be the Name of the Lord!"
He keeps us from all harm.

"Faith of Our Fathers, holy faith"...
A legacy living still;
"O Worship the King," my friend,
And "Press On" to do His will.

"I press toward the mark for the prize
of the high calling of God in Christ Jesus."
(Phil 3:14)

You'll Never Walk Alone

There are rough storms to walk through,
But "You'll Never Walk Alone."
Your loving Lord is with you,
And He takes care of His own.

He gives such "Wonderful Peace."
Let the winds blow and rains come...
"God Will Take Care of You," friend,
For you are safe in His Son!

"I will both lay me down in peace, and sleep:
for thou, LORD, only makest me dwell in safety."
(Ps 4:8)

Sweet Rest

"Beneath the Cross of Jesus,"
All my burdens I lay down,
For they are much too heavy
For me to carry around.

He gives rest to the weary;
We can trust His loving care.
"Take Your Burden to the Lord
and Leave it There."

Jesus said: "Come unto me, all ye that labour
and are heavy laden, and I will give you rest."
(Matt 11:28)

Sweet Hour of Prayer

"I Can Hear My Savior Calling"...
"He Whispers Sweet Peace to Me."
Such a "Sweet Hour of Prayer"...
Lord, "Draw Me Nearer" to Thee.

O God, "Take My Life, Lead Me, Lord,"
"Just a Closer Walk With Thee."
"Make Me a Channel of Blessing,"
Touch some needy soul through me.

"Jesus came and touched them, and said,
Arise, and be not afraid."
(Matt 17:7)

A Glorious Church

The true church is "A Glorious Church,"
"Washed in the blood of the Lamb."
It is the church within the church,
"Redeemed" by the Great I Am.

The bride of Christ, in whom "He Lives,"
Is sacred in every way.
It's sanctified, soon glorified...
Lord, make us holy we pray.

"That he might present it to himself a glorious church,
not having spot, or wrinkle, or any such thing;
but that it should be holy and without blemish."
(Eph 5:27)

Meeting in the Air

"Onward Christian Soldiers,"
Share the gospel with the lost.
"Jesus Is Coming Again,"
Lift "The Banner of the Cross."

"He's Coming Soon" for His church,
Sing His praises everywhere...
O "What a Day That Will Be"!
At that "Meeting in the Air."

"We'll meet the Lord in the air:
and so shall we ever be with the Lord."
(1Thes 4:17b)

Home at Last

"Just Inside the Eastern Gate,"
"Over in the Glory Land,"
We'll cast our crowns at His feet...
And take the Master's hand.

He'll lead to that place prepared,
Where our loved ones wait inside,
Praise God! We'll be "Home at last"...
Forever to abide!

Jesus said: "I go to prepare a place for you...
that where I am, there ye may be also."
(Jn 14:2b, 3b)

He's Everything to Me!

"Now I Belong to Jesus,"
I'm a sheep in His fold.
"He's the Lily of the Valley,"
And Shepherd of my soul.

"O I Want to See Him,"
The One who set me free...
"Hallelujah! What a Savior!"
"He's Everything to Me."

"Looking for that blessed hope,
and the glorious appearing of the great God
and our Saviour Jesus Christ."
(Tit 2:13)

28

I Stand Amazed

When I view God's creation,
The land, the sea, the sky...
"I Stand Amazed" and I say:
What a great God have I!

When I think of salvation,
The cross, His love, His grace...
I sing "Glory to His Name,"
And lift my voice in praise!

"I will praise thee, O Lord, among the people:
I will sing unto thee among the nations."
(Ps 57:9)

Footsteps of Jesus

The "Footsteps of Jesus" lead
To "The Holy City," friends...
All the way to "Beulah Land,"
Where our pilgrim journey ends.

"God Leads Us Along" in love,
As we walk the narrow way...
"Lead On O King Eternal,"
Teach us to "Trust and Obey."

"Lead me in thy truth, and teach me:
for thou art the God of my salvation;
on thee do I wait all the day."
(Ps 25:5)

Victory in Jesus

"Be Still My Soul," "Have Faith in God."
"Faith is the Victory."
I'm "Redeemed" by "Amazing Grace,"
"Thanks to Calvary."

"I Know Whom I Have Believed,"
He set my spirit free!
O sweet "Victory in Jesus,"
Through all eternity!

"Whatsoever is born of God overcometh the world:
and this is the victory that overcometh the world,
even our faith."
(1Jn 5:4)

31

Whiter Than Snow

"Alas, and Did My Savior Bleed"
Precious blood for you and me.
Let's give our best to the Master...
He gave all on Calvary.

"There is Power in the Blood," friend;
It washes "Whiter Than Snow,"
And "Grace, Greater Than Our Sin,"
Sets the heart and soul aglow.

"Purge me with hyssop, and I shall be clean:
wash me, and I shall be whiter than snow."
(Ps 51:7)

My Shepherd

"The Lord's My Shepherd, I'll not want."
He's with me every day;
"I'm Learning to Lean on Jesus,"
And walk His holy way.

"He Leadeth Me! O Blessed Thought!"
His Spirit is my Guide.
Praise God! "It Is Well With My Soul,"
My Shepherd's by my side.

"The LORD is my shepherd; I shall not want."
(Ps 23:1)

Come and Dine

"Every Time I Feel the Spirit"
Calling me to "Come and Dine,"
I pray, "Break Thou the Bread of Life,"
Fill me with manna divine.

The Shepherd has the table spread,
"Whosoever Will May Come."
O "Come to Jesus" and be fed
By the Bread of Life, God's Son.

Jesus said, "I am the bread of life: he that
cometh to me shall never hunger;
and he that believeth on me shall never thirst."
(Jn 6:35)

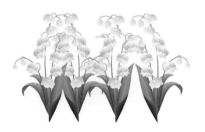

Secure in Him

"From Every Stormy Wind That Blows,"
I have a refuge, safe and warm.
"Trusting Jesus," there is no fear…
"He Hideth My Soul," from the storm.

"Just When I Need Him Most" He's there,
O "Blessed Redeemer" is He!
"Under His Wings," I'm sheltered…
Secure through all eternity!

"He shall cover thee with his feathers, and under
his wings shalt thou trust: his truth shall be
thy shield and buckler."
(Ps 91:4)

Stand Up for Jesus!

Let us "Stand Up for Jesus"
In a crowd, or with just one;
"Lift the Banner of the Cross,"
Share the truth of God the Son.

"We're Marching to Zion," friend,
That glorious Promised Land,
Put on the armor of God...
And in His righteousness stand!

"Watch ye, stand fast in the faith,
quit you like men, be strong."
(1Cor 16:13)

Wondrous Blessings

"Come, Christians, Join to Sing,"
Hearts united in praise;
"Count Your Many Blessings,"
Walk in His holy ways.

"Peace, Peace, Wonderful Peace"
Imparted to the soul;
Thanks to "Jesus, Lamb of God,"
Wondrous blessings unfold.

"Blessed be the God and Father of our Lord
Jesus Christ, who hath blessed us with all
spiritual blessings in heavenly places in Christ."
(Eph 1:3)

The Name of Jesus

"There Is a Name I Love to Hear,"
It's sweet music to the soul.
"Jesus, Name Above All Names,"
Saves from sin and makes us whole.

"There's Just Something About That Name,"
It is glorious to me!
"Take the Name of Jesus with You,"
It can set the captives free.

"And she shall bring forth a son, and thou shalt
call his name JESUS: for he shall
save his people from their sins."
(Matt 1:21)

Such Great Love

"All the Way My Savior Leads Me"
To my home prepared above.
"Day By Day" His Spirit greets me
With His mercy, grace, and love.

"Happy the Home When God is There,"
Kindness and joy fill each heart.
He's "Sweeter As the Days Go By,"
Such great love He doth impart!

"God is love; and he that dwelleth in love
dwelleth in God, and God in him."
(1Jn 4:16b)

Send the Light

O "Send the Light," my Christian friend,
Into this dark world of woe.
The Lord "Jesus is the Lighthouse,"
He'll lead the way as you go.

"Tell it Over Again" to all...
Make the message clear and plain,
And you'll be "Bringing in the Sheaves,"
As you lift His holy Name.

Jesus said: "I am come a light into the world,
that whosoever believeth in me should
not abide in darkness."
(Jn 12:46)

On Calvary's Mountain

The "Blessed Lamb, On Calvary's Mountain,"
Shed His blood, our souls to free.
"He Could Have Called Ten Thousand Angels,"
"O How He Loves You and Me"!

"Praise God From Whom All Blessings Flow,"
The promised Messiah came!
"At The Cross," "Jesus Paid it All,"
O "Glory to His Name"!

"Behold the Lamb of God, which taketh away
the sin of the world."
(Jn 1:29b)

Christ Arose!

"Up From the Grave He Arose,"
To redeem and sanctify.
"Christ the Lord is Risen Today,"
He hears our earnest cry!

O praise be to God, "He Lives."
He's our hope, our victory!
"Because He Lives," we, too, can live,
Forgiven, cleansed, and set free!
"Hallelujah! Christ Arose!"

"The Lord is risen indeed!"
(Lk 24:34a)

42

Sing Praise

Beneath "The Mercy Seat," we kneel
And give praise to Christ the King;
"Thanks to Calvary," we are healed,
And our hearts rejoice and sing.

"Sing Praise to God Who Reigns Above,"
Let us join in one accord:
"Joyful, Joyful, We Adore Thee,"
O sing and worship the Lord!

"Sing unto the LORD, bless his name;
shew forth his salvation from day to day."
(Ps 96:2)

My Redeemer Liveth!

"I Know That My Redeemer Liveth,"
He is with me every day.
"On Jordan's Stormy Banks I Stand,"
Sheltered as He leads the way.

Let us "Crown Him with Many Crowns,"
Our Savior reigns over all!
"Sing Hosanna" to our Great King...
Respond to His gentle call.

"For I know that my redeemer liveth,
and that he shall stand at the latter day
upon the earth."
(Job 19:25)

The Joyful Sound

"When We All Get to Heaven,"
"In the Sweet By and By,"
We'll still be singing praises,
There where no one shall die.

And as we lift our voices,
On Heaven's "Holy Ground,"
"Angels We Have Heard On High"
Will join the joyful sound.

"Blessed is the people that know the
joyful sound: they shall walk, O LORD,
in the light of thy countenance."
(Ps 89:15)

The Cross Made the Difference

"The Old Rugged Cross" of Calvary
Calls out to you and me...
O "Come Just As You Are," my friend,
His blood will set you free!

"The Cross Made the Difference for Me,"
It gave a song to sing...
"Wonderful, Wonderful Jesus,"
Master, Savior, and King.

"In whom we have redemption through his blood,
even the forgiveness of sins."
(Col 1:14)

We Have an Anchor

When the storms of life are raging,
With troubles all around,
"We Have an Anchor" for the soul,
Holding us safe and sound.

"The Anchor Holds" securely, friend,
Whatever trials we face;
There is never a need to fear,
Thanks to "Amazing Grace."

"Which hope we have as an anchor of the soul,
both sure and steadfast."
(Heb 6:19a)

God's Love

"Jesus Loves Me! This I know."
O praise God! "How Can It Be?"
"I Am His and He Is Mine,"
"Day By Day," "He Leadeth Me."

"The Love of God," so amazing,
Will endure throughout all time;
And "One Day," when we reach Glory,
We'll still bask in "Love Divine."

"God is love; and he that dwelleth in love
dwelleth in God, and God in him.
(1Jn 4:16b)

Sweet Peace

Our Lord gives "Peace in the Valley,"
Where the darkness is so grim;
"Perfect Peace" calms the anxious souls
Of all who are trusting Him.

In times of trouble and sorrow,
As we keep our eyes above...
We find, in the darkest hour,
"Sweet Peace, the Gift of God's Love."

"Thou wilt keep him in perfect peace, whose mind is
stayed on thee: because he trusteth in thee."
(Isa 26:3)

What a Fellowship!

"What a Fellowship" is ours,
Abiding in Christ each day!
"May the Circle Be Unbroken"
As we walk in Light and pray.

It's "Sweeter As the Days Go By,"
O "Blest Be the Tie That Binds"!
Nothing Satan has can compare
With what a soul in Christ finds.
"What a Fellowship!"

"If we walk in the light, as he is in the light,
we have fellowship one with another,
and the blood of Jesus Christ his Son
cleanses us of all sin."
(1Jn 1:7)

Hold Fast!

In this world of sin and turmoil,
There is trouble everywhere.
O how "People Need the Lord"
And His tender love and care.

Let us "Hold Fast" to the Lifeline,
Jesus Christ, the Son of God...
Our hope, joy, peace, and victory,
Our Light on this path we trod.

"Let us hold fast the profession of our faith
without wavering; (for he is faithful that promised)"
(Heb 10:23)

I Can Take It

When I meet with troublesome times
And wonder how I'll make it,
I just look to my "Gentle Shepherd"
And I know "I Can Take It."

"He Leadeth Me" over high mountains
And through valleys dark and deep;
The "Spirit of the Living God"
Is right there, my soul to keep.

"The Lord is faithful, who shall stablish you,
and keep you from evil."
(2Th 3:3)

The Light of Life

Praise God for "Heavenly Sunlight,"
Sent from the Father above,
Shining into submissive hearts…
Imparting life, peace, and love.

"The Light of the World is Jesus."
He brightens the darkness grim,
And gives to us the Light of Life…
As we follow close to Him.

Jesus said: "I am the light of the world:
he that followeth me shall not walk in darkness,
but shall have the light of life."
(Jn 8:12)

Take My Hand

Lord, "Thank You for the Valley,"
Where I draw closer to Thee;
It is there, in the dark valley,
You mold and develop me.

And thank you for steep mountains,
For they, too, are in Your plan;
I know "I Need Thee Every Hour,"
O "Precious Lord, Take My Hand."

"I the LORD thy God will hold thy right hand,
saying unto thee, Fear not; I will help thee."
(Isa 41:13)

The Solid Rock

"There's Honey In the Rock," my friend,
Flowing from our Lord's hand...
Completely satisfying souls
Who're lifted "From Sinking Sand."

"On Christ the Solid Rock I Stand,"
Praising God for salvation...
Secure in the "Rock of Ages,"
O "How Firm a Foundation"!

"He is the Rock, his work is perfect:
for all his ways are judgment: a God of
truth and without iniquity, just and right is he."
(Deut 32:4)

Just As I Am

"Just As I Am," broken and tossed,
"Jesus, I Come" to Thee.
Kneeling at "The Old Rugged Cross,"
I find such victory!

"Wonderful, Wonderful Jesus,"
As I bow before Thee,
"Sweet Peace, the Gift of God's Love,"
Fills my spirit with glee.

"Great peace have they which love thy law,
and nothing shall offend them."
(Ps 119:165)

Let's Live Lives of Purity

"Precious, Precious Blood of Jesus,"
The pure blood that frees us,
Cleanses our hearts from every sin...
Making us pure within.

Let us be an example, friend,
Never yielding to sin,
But in "Faith, Hope, and Charity,"
Let's live lives of purity.

"Let no man despise thy youth; but be thou an
example of the believers, in word, in conversation,
in charity, in spirit, in faith, in purity."
(1Tim 4:12)

Safe in Him!

My friend, when we "Come to Jesus,"
Laying everything down…
We enter "The Haven of Rest,"
And there's no sweeter ground.

It is "The Hallelujah Side,"
Angels are all about…
We're "Safe in the Arms of Jesus,"
No man can pluck us out!

Jesus said, "I give unto them eternal life;
and they shall never perish, neither shall
any man pluck them out of my hand."
(Jn 10:28)

Set My Soul Afire

"Blessed Be the Name of the Lord,"
Jesus, our Savior and King;
Draw me "Nearer My God to Thee,"
Till there's "Nothing Between."

"Jesus, the Very Thought of Thee"
Ignites a flame deep within;
Oh, just "Set My Soul Afire, Lord,"
And use me some soul to win.

"I heard the voice of the Lord, saying,
Whom shall I send, and who will go for us?
Then said I, Here am I; send me."
(Isa 6:8)

Jesus is Coming Again

Friend, "Jesus is Coming Again,"
Of that we're very sure!
Let us live for His glory...
Lives that are clean and pure.

"One Day," we'll see Him coming
In the clouds of the air;
His hand holds the Book of Life...
Be sure your name is there!

"Whosoever was not found written
in the book of life was cast into
the lake of fire."
(Rev 20:15)

I'm Going Home

O friend, "This World Is Not My Home,"
"I Am a Pilgrim" here;
"I Am Bound For the Promised Land,"
Where no one sheds a tear.

And "When They Ring Those Golden Bells,"
"I'll Fly Away" with glee!
O Praise God! "We Shall See the King."
"What a Day That Will Be!"
"Hallelujah! I'm Going Home."

"And so shall we ever be with the Lord."
(1Th 4:17b)

March On!

Let's march "Onward, Christian Soldiers,"
"Till Jesus Comes Again."
"Fight the Good Fight With All Thy Might,"
He has a perfect plan.

"Take the Name Of Jesus With You,"
"Send the Light" everywhere;
There is "Victory In Jesus,"
And you're safe in His care...
March On!

"Thou therefore endure hardness as a
good soldier of Jesus Christ."
(2Tim 2:3)

The Royal Telephone

Our Father has provided
"The Royal Telephone,"
And He will always answer
From His Majestic Throne.

He's the Great Almighty God,
Yet He makes Himself known
Through sweet communication…
"The Royal Telephone."

"He shall call upon me, and I will answer him:
I will be with him in trouble; I will
deliver him and honour him."
(Ps 91:15)

He Never Failed Me Yet!

Friend, when your heart is broken,
There's just one thing to do;
"Take It to the Lord in Prayer"...
"He Will Fix It For You."

And when troubles and trials come,
You need not fear or fret;
"God Will Make A Way" for you...
"He Never Failed Me Yet!"

"Be strong and of good courage, fear not...
for the LORD thy God, he it is that doth go with thee;
he will not fail thee, nor forsake thee."
(Deut 31:6)

64

Union in Glory

Friend, we are "On the Battlefield,"
God's Spirit is our Sword;
Our victory is guaranteed
With Jesus Christ our Lord!

"When We All Get To Heaven,"
"In the Sweet Forever,"
'Twill be a union in Glory
Not one thing can sever!

"Fight the good fight of faith,
lay hold on eternal life, whereunto thou art
also called, and hast professed a good profession
before many witnesses."
(1Tim 6:12)

Where Healing Waters Flow

Lord, keep me following Thee,
No matter where others go,
For I always want to be
"Where the Healing Waters Flow."

If I start to drift away,
In this sinful world below,
Bring me back to Thee, I pray,
"Where the Healing Waters Flow."

"He maketh me to lie down in green pastures:
he leadeth me beside the still waters."
(Ps 23:2)

I Shall Not Be Moved!

"I Am Resolved" to follow Christ
With the faithful few;
"Just When I Need Him Most," He's there
To carry me through.

"Standing On the Promises,"
Rough times are made smooth.
Planted on the "Rock of Ages,"
"I Shall Not Be Moved"!

"He only is my rock and my salvation:
he is my defence; I shall not be moved."
(Ps 62:6)

Bound For Glory!

I'm headed for that glorious place
"Where We'll Never Grow Old"...
A land of beauty, love, and grace,
That sweet "Home of the Soul."

Yes, "This Train Is Bound For Glory,"
I do hope you're on board...
Come, let's "Sing the Wondrous Story,"
Rejoice, and praise the Lord.

"Rejoicing in hope; patient in tribulation;
continuing instant in prayer."
(Rom 12:12)

Sunshine in My Soul

There's "Sunshine in My Soul Today"!
I know my Lord's with me...
"He Keeps Me Singing" on my way,
And sets my spirit free.

"In My Heart There Rings a Melody,"
I just can't help but sing...
"Sing O Sing Of My Redeemer,"
Jesus, Savior and King!

"Sing unto him, sing psalms unto him,
talk ye of all his wondrous works."
(1Ch 16:9)

The Other Shore

"When We Reach the Other Shore,"
Where the streets are made of gold…
We'll enjoy the "Unclouded Day,"
"While the Endless Ages Roll."

"The Holy City" will be lit
With the glory of our Lord…
We'll sing in "Heavenly Sunlight,"
Joined with saints in one accord.

"The city had no need of the sun, neither of the moon
to shine in it: for the glory of God did lighten it;
and the Lamb is the light thereof."
(Rev 21:23)

God Will Take Care of You

"Got Any Rivers to Cross?"
Any mountains to climb?
Friend, "God Will Take Care of You"...
Your heart, your soul, your mind.

"Turn Your Eyes Upon Jesus,"
The Shepherd knows His own;
"His Love Lights the Way" for you...
Trust Him to lead you on.

"The LORD is good, a stronghold in the day
of trouble; and he knoweth them
that trust in him."
(Nah 1:7)

Let the Hallelujahs Roll!

"I Know Whom I Have Believed,"
His "Precious Blood" set me free!
"More About Jesus Let Me Learn,"
For "He's Everything to Me."

"Since Jesus Came Into My Heart,"
"It is Well With My Soul"!
In Him is "Joy Unspeakable"...
"Let the Hallelujahs Roll!"

"Whom having not seen, ye love; in whom,
though now ye see him not, yet believing,
ye rejoice with joy unspeakable
and full of glory."
(1Pet 1:8)

72

Beneath the Cross

"Beneath the Cross of Jesus,"
We're "Redeemed" and made whole;
"Nothing But the Blood" can cleanse
And purify the soul.

"The Love of God" is so great,
Not one thing can compare!
"Whosoever Will May Come,"
And He will meet you there...
"Beneath the Cross."

"Unto Him that loved us, and washed us
from our sins in his own blood...to him be
glory and dominion for ever and ever."
(Rev 1:5b, 6b)

Keep on Singing

Friend, "The Old Account Was Settled"
"Down On My Knees" in prayer,
And "Some Glad Day" "I'll Fly Away"...
I hope you'll "Meet Me There."

We'll sing, "Holy, Holy, Holy,"
There in the Promised Land;
"Until Then," let's keep on singing...
Knowing God has a plan.

"Speaking to yourselves in psalms and hymns
and spiritual songs, singing and making melody
in your heart to the Lord."
(Eph 5:19)

Words of Life

Such "Wonderful Words of Life"
In God's Holy Book!
Friend, If you haven't seen the Light,
Take another look.

The message is clear and plain,
"Jesus Paid it All"!
Precious words of eternal life...
O hear His tender call.

"Then said Jesus to the twelve, Will ye also go away?
Then Simon Peter answered him, Lord,
to whom shall we go? Thou hast the
words of eternal life."
(Jn 6:67-68)

His Hands

"He's Got the Whole World in His Hands,"
Each mountain, valley, and sea;
And in every situation,
He's right there with you and me.

Friend, "His Eye is On the Sparrow,"
He cares for each little bird;
"His Hands" can move mountains we face,
And in valleys undergird.

"In his hand are the deep places of the earth: the
strength of the hills is his also. The sea is his,
and he made it: and his hands formed the dry land."
(Ps 95:4-5)

In His Presence

"In the Presence of Jehovah,"
Peace and joy flood the soul;
His "Sweet, Sweet Spirit" warms the heart
Of His sheep in the fold.

Are you outside the pasture, friend,
Still in darkness bound?
"There's Room At the Cross for You,"
Where lost sheep are found...
In His Presence.

"Glory and honour are in his presence;
strength and gladness are in his place."
(1Ch 16:27)

I'll Let It Shine

Oh, "I Love To Tell the Story"
Of Jesus Christ my King...
How He left His home in Glory,
Eternal life to bring.

I'll shine "This Little Light of Mine,"
Till heaven's gates unfold;
I just can't help but let it shine...
"There's Sunshine In My Soul."

Jesus said: "Let your light so shine before men,
that they may see your good works,
and glorify your Father which is in heaven."
(Matt 5:16)

Search Me, O God

"Search Me, O God," cleanse my heart,
"Make Me a Blessing" I pray.
"Sweet Holy Spirit," "Breathe on Me,"
Show me Thy will and way.

"O Spirit of the Living God,"
"My Faith Looks Up to Thee,"
LORD, "Take My Life, and Let it Be"
Ever yielded to Thee.

"Search me, O God, and know my heart: try me, and
know my thoughts: And see if there be any wicked
way in me, and lead me in the way everlasting."
(Ps 139:23-24)

Sweeter As the Days Go By

"The Longer I Serve Him, the Sweeter He Grows,"
"He is So Precious to Me"!
And "It Gets Sweeter As the Days Go By,"
"Thanks to Calvary."

Yes, "Every Day With Jesus" is sweeter,
For "He is Faithful to Me."
"I'm Learning to Lean" on Christ, my Savior...
He is my victory!

"How sweet are thy words unto my taste!
yea, sweeter than honey to my mouth!"
(Ps 119:103)

We Shall See the King

Praise God! "We Shall See the King"
"Some Sweet Day, By and By"...
"Somewhere Over the Rainbow"
We'll join Him in the sky.

"The Eastern Gate" will open wide
On that glorious day,
And He will greet us at the Door,
Clothed in His bright array... Hallelujah!
"We Shall See the King."

"And he hath on his vesture
and on his thigh a name written,
KING OF KINGS AND LORD OF LORDS."
(Rev 19:16)

Keep on the Sunny Side

We can "Keep on the Sunny Side,"
Though storm clouds are all around;
"God Put a Rainbow in the Cloud,"
And it can always be found.

When we walk through the dark valley,
Let us look up toward the sky...
And "Keep on the Sunny Side," friend;
Our redemption draweth nigh.

Jesus said: "And when these things begin to come
to pass, then look up, and lift up your heads;
for your redemption draweth nigh."
(Lk 21:28)

Pass It On

"We Have Heard the Joyful Sound,"
"Spread, O Spread the Mighty Word."
"Pass It On" to all around...
No greater message is heard!

We see so much disaster!
"Throw Out the Lifeline," my friend,
"Give of Your Best to the Master"...
Share the gospel with all men.

Jesus said: "Go ye into all the world,
and preach the gospel to every creature."
(Mark 16:15)

Faith of Our Fathers

"Faith of Our Fathers living still"
Through every generation...
Faith that troubles and trials can't kill,
O "How Firm a Foundation"!

Thank You, God, for "The Solid Rock,"
Upon which our faith is built.
Thank you for hearing when we knock,
And cleansing from sin and guilt.

"Let us hold fast the profession of our faith
without wavering; (for he is faithful that promised.)"
(Heb 10:23)

Why Do I Sing?

"Why Do I Sing About Jesus?"
He's my Redeemer and Friend!
"Jesus Is All the World To Me,"
My Deliverer from sin.

How could I not sing His praises?
He's my LORD and Mighty King!
"All That Thrills My Soul Is Jesus"...
Lift your voice with me and sing!

"Sing unto God, ye kingdoms of the earth;
O sing praises unto the Lord; Se-lah."
(Ps 68:32)

Stand Up!

"O Come, All Ye Faithful,"
"Dare to Be a Daniel."
"Stand Up for Jesus," friend,
His powerful message send.

"People Need the Lord,"
Let's proclaim His Holy Word;
"Onward Christian Soldiers,"
Armed with the Spirit's sword…
Stand Up!

"And take the helmet of salvation, and the sword
of the Spirit, which is the word of God."
(Eph 6:17)

Standing on the Solid Rock

"I'm Standing on the Solid Rock,"
The only sure foundation.
Jesus, Rock of all the ages,
Secures our great salvation.

Praise God! "I Shall Not Be Moved"
When trials and troubles come.
"The Anchor Holds" through every storm…
When grounded in God's Son.

"He only is my rock and my salvation:
he is my defence; I shall not be moved."
(Ps 62:6)

God Leads Us Along

Life's journey can seem long and hard,
And sometimes we slip and fall;
But "God Leads His Dear Children Along,"
He's right there, "Through It All.

"O How He Loves You and Me," friend,
He corrects us when we're wrong;
"Softly and Tenderly" He calls...
And imparts a joyful song.

"Teach me to do thy will; for thou art my God:
thy spirit is good; lead me into the land
of uprightness."
(Ps 143:10)

Too Late to Pray

Christ's return is very near, friend,
"He's Coming Soon" in the air.
"When the Roll Is Called Up Yonder,"
Will your name be written there?

"Shall We Gather At the River"
On "That Glad Reunion Day"?
O "What a Gathering That Will Be"!
But for some… "Too Late to Pray."

Jesus said: "Take ye heed, watch and pray:
for ye know not when the time is."
(Mk 13:33)

Such Great Blessings

"Every Time I Feel the Spirit
Moving in my heart I pray,"
Lord, "Take My Life and Let it Be"
A useful vessel today.

"Joy Unspeakable" fills my heart,
Since, by grace, He made me whole;
"He Keeps Me Singing" "Day By Day,"
As such great blessings unfold.

"Blessed be the God and Father of our Lord
Jesus Christ; who hath blessed us with all
spiritual blessings in heavenly places in Christ."
(Eph 1:3)

The Love of God

"The Love of God" is amazing!
It's love beyond compare.
There, on that "Old Rugged Cross,"
All our sins He did bear.

His "Love Lifted Me" from darkness
Into marvelous Light…
"I Just Can't Praise Him Enough"
For eternal life so bright.

"For the wages of sin is death, but the gift
of God is eternal life through Jesus Christ our Lord."
(Rom 6:23)

Blessed Be the Name

"Blessed Be the Name of the Lord."
"Hallelujah! What a Savior!"
"He Ransomed Me" "At Calvary,"
Now I live in His favor.

"And Can It Be That I Should Gain"
Life with Him forevermore?
"Great Is His Faithfulness," my friend!
I'll be there on Heaven's Shore.

"God is faithful, by whom ye were called unto
the fellowship of his Son Jesus Christ our Lord."
(1Cor 1:9)

In the Garden

It's so precious "In the Garden,"
When we come to God in prayer,
Or wherever that special place,
He will always meet us there.

"In the Presence of Jehovah,"
We learn His will and way,
And we can better serve Him, friend,
When we have knelt to pray.

Jesus said: "When thou prayest, enter into
thy closet, and when thou hast shut the door,
pray to thy Father which is in secret;
and thy Father which seeth in secret
shall reward thee openly."
(Matt 6:6)

Christ Is All I Need

"Christ Is All I Need" in this world
To satisfy my soul.
He is the Light unto my path,
He leads me in His fold.

"He's All I Need" to be joyful,
Even in troubled days.
He's the Way, the Truth, and the Life,
I lift my voice in praise!

"I will bless the LORD at all times:
his praise shall continually be in my mouth."
(Ps 34:1)

Living For Jesus

"Beulah Land, I'm longing for you,"
Land "Where We'll Never Grow Old,"
Longing to see my Shepherd's face…
And be made perfectly whole.

"Until Then," I will "Follow On,"
"Living For Jesus" each day…
Giving thanks, singing His praises,
Planting seeds along the way.

"He died for all, that they which live should not
henceforth live unto themselves, but unto him
which died for them, and rose again."
(2Cor 5:15)

Our Savior Lives!

"I Serve A Risen Savior," friend,
"He Is So Precious to Me"!
"He Keeps Me Singing" every day…
"Let Him Have His Way With Thee."

The "Holy Bible, Book Divine,"
Tells how "He Arose" that day.
Hallelujah! Our Savior lives!
The stone was rolled away!

"He is not here; for he is risen, as he said.
Come, see the place where our Lord lay."
(Matt 28:6)

Keep Me True

"I've Found a Friend who is all to me,"
He saved me by His grace.
"Jesus, the Very Thought of Thee"
Lifts up my heart in praise.

"All the Way My Savior Leads Me"
To "Higher Ground" each day.
"Wonderful, Wonderful Jesus,"
"Keep Me True," Lord, I pray.

"Faithful is he that calleth you,
who also will do it."
(1Thes 5:24)

The Good Fight

"Who is on the Lord's Side?"
"Soldiers of Christ, Arise!"
"Fight the Good Fight of Faith,"
As you look toward the skies.

"Onward Christian Soldiers,"
The time is growing late;
"When the Battle's Over,"
O how we'll celebrate!

"Fight the good fight of faith, lay hold
on eternal life, whereunto thou art also
called, and hast professed a good profession
among many witnesses."
(1Tim 6:12)

Let Freedom Ring

We sing, "Stars and Stripes Forever,"
And "God Bless the U.S.A.,"
But do we deserve His blessings?
Have we walked His Holy way?

Many fought and died for freedom,
And we thank them every one;
Let us honor them by serving
The Lord Jesus Christ, God's Son...
And "Let Freedom Ring."

"Blessed is the nation whose God is the Lord."
(Ps 33:12a)

I'd Rather Have Jesus

"I'd Rather Have Jesus," my friend,
Than money, houses, or land,
Cabins in the mountains,
Condos on the sand.

"Nothing but the Blood of Jesus"
Can purify the soul,
Give peace and joy within the heart,
And secure us in the fold...
"I'd Rather Have Jesus than anything!"

Jesus said: "Where your treasure is,
there will your heart be also."
(Matt 6: 21)

He's All I Need

We need no worldly entertainment,
Nor the pleasures of sin,
For our deepest needs are satisfied
When Jesus dwells within.

"Christ Is All I Need, He's All I Need,"
"He's Everything to Me."
He is "The Lily Of the Valley,"
Our Life, our Victory.

"Thou wilt shew me the path of life:
in thy presence is fulness of joy: at thy
right hand there are pleasures for evermore."
(Ps 16:11)

Shine the Light

"We've a Story to Tell," my friend,
  If in Christ we abide;
 "Go Tell it on the Mountain,"
Shine His message far and wide.

O "Send the Light" into this world
  Steeped in immorality;
 "The Love of God" reaches the lost,
  Cleansing for eternity.

Jesus said: "No man, when he hath lighted a
candle, putteth it in a secret place, neither under
a bushel, but on a candlestick, that they
which come in may see the light."
(Lk 11:33)

102

Through It All

Life is just not always easy,
There are valleys we must face;
But, "Through It All," our God is there,
Undergirding by His grace.

"Have Faith in God," "Trust and Obey,"
And when you can't understand,
Lift your voice and give Him praise...
Your God has a perfect plan!

"As for God, his way is perfect: the word
of the LORD is tried: he is a buckler to all
those that trust in him."
(Ps 18:30)

More About Jesus

Lord, "As the Deer" thirsts for water,
My soul thirsts for Thee.
O Holy Spirit, "Fill My Cup"
Till Christ is seen in me.

Draw me "Nearer My God to Thee,"
Make my heart pure I pray.
"More About Jesus Let Me Learn,"
Teach me Thy Holy way.

Jesus said: "Take my yoke upon you, and learn of me;
for I am meek and lowly in heart: and ye shall
find rest unto your souls."
(Matt 11:29)

Be Still My Soul

"Be Still My Soul" and you will know
Your Holy God is there!
You'll sense a "Blessed Quietness" flow
With peace beyond compare.

"Softly and Tenderly" He'll speak
His will and way to you.
You are sheltered "Under His Wings,"
He'll always see you through...
Just be still!

"Be still and know that I am God: I will be exalted
among the heathen, I will be exalted in the earth."
(Ps 46:10)

All Sufficient

Lord, "My Faith Looks Up To Thee"
No matter where the road winds...
In those times of tragedy,
Or fair days when the sun shines;

"I Need Thee Every Hour,"
Whatever my lot may be...
Thy grace, mercy, and power
Are all sufficient for me.

"Not that we are sufficient of ourselves
to think any thing as of ourselves;
but our sufficiency is of God."
(2Cor 3:5)

It Won't Be Long

Christian, "Press On, It Won't Be Long"
Till that "Meeting in the Air,"
We'll see Christ coming in the clouds
And rise to meet Him there.

There will be "No Tears in Heaven,"
No more suffering or pain;
Only peace, joy, and happiness...
A place of eternal gain.
"Press On, It Won't Be Long."

"And God shall wipe away all tears from their eyes;
and there shall be no more death, neither sorrow,
nor crying, neither shall there be anymore pain:
for the former things are passed away."
(Rev 21:4)

When You Reach the End

When you reach the end of your way
And feel you can't go on,
"The Savior is Waiting" to help...
He will make Himself known.

Friend, "Turn Your Eyes Upon Jesus,"
He knows just what to do!
"From Sinking Sand He Lifted Me"...
He'll do the same for you.

The LORD said: "Call upon me in the day of trouble:
I will deliver thee, and thou shalt glorify me."
(Ps 50:15)

Our God Reigns!

"Wonderful, Wonderful Jesus,"
Loving Shepherd, and Great King!
"Blessed Be the Name of the Lord,"
Let's lift our voices and sing:

"All Hail the Power of Jesus Name,"
Precious "Name Above All Names."
"O For a Thousand Tongues to Sing,"
Hallelujah! "Our God Reigns"!

"God reigneth over the heathen: God sitteth upon
the throne of his holiness."
(Ps 47:8)

Thou Art Worthy!

O Lord my God, "Thou Art Worthy"...
Worthy of honor and praise.
"I Stand Amazed" at Thy greatness
And all of Thy perfect ways.

In awe I sing, "How Great Thou Art"...
Creator of all the earth;
Yet our loving Friend and Shepherd;
Nothing compares with Thy worth!

"GREAT is the LORD, and greatly to be
praised in the city of our God, in the mountain
of his holiness...For this God is our God for ever
and ever: he will be our guide even unto death."
(Ps 48:1, 14)

110

It Took a Miracle!

In the beginning, when God spoke,
Heaven and earth did appear;
And when He said, "Let there be light,"
There was light, bright and clear...
"It Took a Miracle!"

When His Spirit drew us to Christ
And redeemed our sinful soul,
He imparted new spiritual life
As He cleansed and made us whole...
"It Took a Miracle!"

"O Lord GOD, thou hast begun to shew thy servant
thy greatness and thy mighty hand:
for what God is there in heaven or in earth,
that can do according to thy works,
and according to thy might"?
(Deut 3:24)

111

No Greater Love

"The Love of God" is much greater
Than any other love.
Everywhere that we look we see
Such blessings from above!

"O Love That Wilt Not Let Me Go,"
Though I be tempest tossed;
Friend, what greater love could we know
Than was shown "At The Cross"?
No Greater Love!

"Greater love hath no man than this,
that a man lay down his life for his friends."
(Jn 15:13)

A Song In My Heart

Once the world was dark and dreary,
The road so hard to face;
Then "He Put a Song in My Heart"
And lifted me by grace.

"In My Heart There Rings a Melody,"
My God has set me free!
I'll sing and magnify His Name
Through all eternity.

"I will praise the name of God with a song,
and will magnify him with thanksgiving."
(Ps 69:30)

We Shall Behold Him!

"One Day," "In the Sweet By and By,"
When this life on earth is o'er,
"We Shall Behold Him," King of kings,
And rejoice for evermore.

"Until Then," we're "Living by Faith,"
Trusting Him every day;
"What a Friend We Have In Jesus,"
He is with us all the way.

"For he hath said, I will never leave thee,
nor forsake thee."
(Heb 13:5b)

114

We Can Trust Him

"Farther Along" we'll understand
The troublesome times we face;
For now let's trust His sovereign hand,
And rest in His loving grace.

"God Will Take Care of You," my friend,
Through every dark stormy vale;
You can always trust in Him...
Our Mighty God will not fail!

"Be strong and of a good courage, fear not...
for the LORD thy God, he it is that doth
go with thee; he will not fail thee, nor forsake thee."
(Deut 31:6)

Thanks to Amazing Grace

"He Leadeth Me, O blessed thought,"
To that great Home above;
From chains of bondage He freed me...
Such mercy and "Such Love"!

With joy I'll lift my voice and sing
Till I behold His face;
Praise God, "I'm a Child of the King,"
Thanks to "Amazing Grace."

"Not by works of righteousness which we have done,
but according to his mercy he saved us,
by the washing of regeneration,
and renewing of the Holy Ghost."
(Tit 3:5)

116

The Hope of Glory

"In Times Like These You need a Savior."
Jesus came to save from sin!
"Are You Washed In the Blood of the Lamb?"
Time is short and soon will end.

"The Holy City" awaits us, friend,
When our Lord we come to know;
Christ in us is the hope of Glory...
Let us be ready to go!

"Christ in you the hope of glory;
Whom we preach, warning every man,
and teaching every man in all wisdom."
(Col 1:27b-28a)

Sound the Battle Cry

Let us "Sound the Battle Cry,"
The time is growing late;
O "Soldiers of Christ, Arise,"
We'll soon see Heaven's gate.

There's "Victory in Jesus,"
He's our strong faithful Guide;
March "Onward Christian Soldiers,"
We're on the winning side!

"Thou therefore endure hardness,
as a good soldier of Jesus Christ."
(2Tim 2:3)

O Happy Day!

"O Happy Day" when we reach Glory,
All our loved ones gathered round,
We'll still sing the wondrous story
There on Heaven's "Holy Ground."

Free from trouble, sorrow and pain,
O "What a Day that Will Be"!
With Jesus, our King, we shall reign...
Singing praise eternally...
"O Happy Day!"

"There shall be no night there; and they
need no candle, neither light of the sun;
for the Lord God giveth them light:
and they shall reign for ever and ever."
(Rev 22:5)

Just a Prayer Away!

When you're feeling sad and weary,
There's a remedy for you...
Just "Turn Your Eyes Upon Jesus,"
And the sun will shine right through.

"Trusting Jesus" with all your heart,
And living for Him each day,
Brings "Joy unspeakable," my friend,
And He's just a prayer away!

"I will lift up mine eyes unto the hills,
from whence cometh my help."
(Ps 121:1)

No Need to Fear!

In this world of heartache and pain,
"We Have an Anchor" that holds.
Let the storms come with wind and rain...
We're safe whatever unfolds.

No need to fear the worst of foes
When Jesus has saved our souls;
"From Every Stormy Wind That Blows,"
He whispers: "The Anchor Holds"...
No Need to Fear!

"Which hope we have as an anchor of the soul,
both sure and steadfast, which entereth into
that within the veil."
(Heb 6:19)

O The Wonder of It All!

From Heaven to earth Jesus came,
To redeem us from the fall.
He bore all of our sin and shame,
"O The Wonder of It All"!

He satisfies the heart and soul,
And He heals the troubled mind;
"Softly and Tenderly" He calls
To the hungry, "Come and Dine"...
"O The Wonder of It All!"

"For he satisfieth the longing soul,
and filleth the hungry soul with goodness."
(Ps 107:9)

Into His Light

Into this dark world, our Lord came...
The true Light that lights the heart;
Through "Jesus, the Light of the World,"
We're lifted out of the dark.

"Seek Ye First the Kingdom of God,"
And be brought into His Light;
Your path will be lit with His Word...
And your journey will be bright.

"Thy word is a lamp unto my feet,
and a light unto my path."
(Ps 119:105)

On the Rock I Stand!

"I Was Sinking Deep in Sin,"
With no anchor for my soul,
"Then Jesus Came" and lifted me...
"He Touched Me" and made me whole.

My soul is anchored in my Lord,
And I am safe in His hand;
"My Faith Has Found a Resting Place,"
On "The Solid Rock I stand"!

"He is the Rock, his work is perfect:
for all his ways are judgment: a God of truth
and without iniquity, just and right is he."
(Deut 32:4)

All In His Name

"Take this Whole World, but Give Me Jesus,"
The perfect Lamb of God who came;
O "Wonderful, Wonderful Jesus,"
"There's Just Something About That Name"!

I will praise His Name forevermore...
Hallelujah! His blood frees us!
Love and forgiveness, grace and mercy,
"It's All In the Name of Jesus."

"I will praise thee, O Lord my God,
with all my heart: and I will glorify
thy name for evermore."
(Ps 86:12)

Precious Lord, Take My Hand

"Precious Lord, Take My Hand,"
"I Need Thee Every Hour."
Lead me through the valley,
Sustain me by Thy power.

And on the mountain high,
In days sunny and fair,
"Precious Lord, Take My Hand,"
For I still need Thee there.

"Lead me in thy truth, and teach me:
for thou art the God of my salvation;
on thee do I wait all the day."
(Ps 25:5)

Calvary Covers it All

All our sin, past, present, future...
"Calvary Covers it All."
O "The Love of God" our Savior!
He tore down the middle wall.

The redeemed now commune with Him,
No more sin to separate.
We are "Bound for the Promised Land,"
O what Glory doth await!
Yes, "Calvary Covers it All."

"For he is our peace, who hath made both one,
and hath broken down the middle wall
of partition between us."
(Eph 2:14)

Lift Him Up

Let's raise "The Banner of The Cross"
For all the world to see...
Christ is the way, the truth, the life,
He sets the sinner free.

O "Send The Light," the gospel Light,
The message is so clear,
Lift Him up before it's too late...
His return is very near!

Jesus said: "And I, if I be lifted up
from the earth,
will draw all men unto me."
(Jn 12:32)

The God of Israel

"Blessed Be the God of Israel,"
He's in complete control!
"Great is His Faithfulness" each day
To the sheep in His fold.

O "Fear Not, Rejoice and Be Glad,"
He is working His plan.
"God Will Take Care of You," my friend,
He holds you in His hand.

"Ye that love the LORD, hate evil:
he preserveth the souls of his saints;
he delivereth them out of the hand of the wicked."
(Ps 97:10)

Safe in His Arms

"O God, Our Help in Ages Past,"
Our world is filled with tension!
On Thee all our burdens we cast...
Trusting Your intervention.

We hear of wars, rumors of wars,
Yet we know we need not fear.
We're "Safe in the Arms of Jesus,"
And His coming is so near.

Jesus said: "And when ye hear of wars and rumours
of wars, be ye not troubled: for such things
must needs be; but the end shall not be yet."
(Mk 13:7)

I Still Shall Sing!

"I Will Sing of the Mercies"
Of my Redeemer and Friend.
"He Put a Song in My Heart"
That satisfies within.

"I Will Sing the Wondrous Story"
Till those golden bells ring;
And when He takes me to Glory,
Praise God! I still shall sing!

"I will sing of thy power; yea, I will sing aloud
of thy mercy in the morning: for thou hast been
my defence and refuge in the day of my trouble."
(Ps 59:16)

Thank You, Lord!

"Sweetly, Lord, We Have Heard Thee Calling,"
Drawing us unto Thee;
Keep us following ever so close...
Till Heaven's Home we see.

And "When the Roll is Called Up Yonder,"
Our names will be right there;
Thou hast saved us by "Amazing Grace,"
And kept us in Thy care.
"Thank You, Lord, For Saving My Soul."

"For by grace are ye saved through faith;
and that not of yourselves: it is the gift of God:
Not of works, lest any man should boast."
(Eph 2:8-9)

Give Us Christians

"God, Give Us Christian Homes" we pray,
Homes that center around Thee;
And give us true Christian churches,
Where lost souls can be set free.

May our hearts be pure and humble,
Ready Thy Truth to proclaim;
As we share in our daily lives,
May we lift the Savior's Name...
Jesus! What a "Precious Name"!

"That at the name of Jesus every knee should bow,
of things in heaven, and things in earth,
and things under the earth."
(Phil 2:10)

133

Jesus, the Light

Lord "Jesus, the Light of the World,"
Our Guide through the dark night,
Thou art the lamp unto our feet...
Help us "Walk in the Light."

"How Brightly Beams the Morning Star,"
Filling our hearts with praise;
With joy we sing, "How Great Thou Art,"
And holy anthems raise...
Unto Thee, "The Light of the World."

"Then spake Jesus again unto them, saying,
I am the light of the world: he that followeth
me shall not walk in darkness,
but shall have the light of life."
(Jn 8:12)

Keep Looking Up!

"There Is Sunshine in My Soul Today,"
Sweet "Heavenly Sunlight,"
It's with me as I "Trust and Obey,"
Glowing ever so bright.

We could all sink like Peter of old,
If we just look around,
But when we keep our eyes on the Lord…
Nothing can get us down.
Keep Looking Up!

Jesus said: "And when these things begin to
come to pass, then look up, and lift up your heads;
for your redemption draweth nigh."
(Lk 21:28)

His Blood Set Us Free!

"Jesus Loves Me, this I know"...
"He Touched Me and made me whole."
"He Keeps Me Singing as I go,"
Shining His Light in my soul.

"Hallelujah! What a Savior!"
"He's Pouring out Blessings on Me."
Let us rejoice, my Christian friend...
His precious blood set us free!

Jesus said: "If the Son therefore shall make you free,
ye shall be free indeed."
(Jn 8:36)

To God Be the Glory

"Jesus, the Very Thought of Thee"
Lifts my heart in joyful praise!
"O Happy Day" when You saved me
And revealed Thy holy ways.

"I Love to Tell the Story,"
How, by grace, You set me free;
I'll sing "To God Be the Glory"
Throughout all eternity!

"To the only wise God our Saviour,
be glory and majesty, dominion and power,
both now and ever. Amen."
(Jude 1:25)

137

Worship In Reverence!

"Come, We That Love the Lord,"
Let us worship in reverence...
"Holy, Holy, Holy" is He!
We're humbled in His presence.

"O To Be Like Thee," precious Lord,
Pure and Holy every day;
Draw us "Nearer, My God, to Thee,"
Help us walk Thy righteous way...
And worship in reverence!

"God is greatly to be feared in the assembly
of the saints, and to be had in reverence of
all them that are about him."
(Ps 89:7)

Serve and Pray

Sometimes, when I see the problems,
"I Feel Like Traveling On,"
But I know our God has a plan...
Gospel seed is being sown.

We'll see "The Land of Perfect Day"
When all the sheep are brought in;
But "Until Then" let's serve and pray...
Reaching out, the lost to win.

Jesus said: "Go ye into all the world, and preach
the gospel to every creature."
(Mk 16:15)

He's Coming Soon

When the world is in such turmoil,
And I wonder what will be,
I hear a still small voice within...
"He Whispers Sweet Peace to Me."

Let's "Hold to God's Unchanging Hand"
Whatever takes place around;
Christ, our Lord, is coming again...
Soon we'll hear the trumpet sound.
Hallelujah! "He's Coming Soon."

Jesus Said: "And If I go and prepare a place
for you, I will come again, and receive you
unto myself; that where I am, there ye may be also."
(Jn 14:3)

Lead Me to Calvary

If ever I begin to stray,
"Lead Me to Calvary."
I want to walk uprightly,
Till my LORD'S face I see.

His grace and strength are sufficient,
His Spirit dwells within;
"It Is Glory to Walk With Him,"
My God and dearest Friend!

"For the LORD God is a sun and shield:
the LORD will give grace and glory:
no good thing will he withhold from
them that walk uprightly."
(Ps 84:11)

The Time is Now!

"Jesus is Tenderly Calling,"
O come to Him today!
"There's Room at the Cross for you," friend,
Where sins are washed away.

Place your hand in "The Nail-Scarred Hand,"
You'll find salvation there.
O come to Christ while there's still time,
Bow before Him in prayer…
The time is now!

"Behold, now is the accepted time;
behold, now is the day of salvation."
(2Cor 6:2b)

He Is Leading the Way!

Whenever I get discouraged,
I look above and pray,
And the Comforter assures me
"He Is Leading the Way."

How I love that small voice within
"Whispering Hope" to me.
"His Eye Is On the Sparrow," friend,
He hears our every plea...
"He Is Leading the Way!"

Jesus said: "And when he putteth forth
his own sheep, he goeth before them,
and the sheep follow him: for they know his voice."
(Jn 10:4)

A Land Fairer Than Day

"There's a Land that is Fairer than Day."
No other place can compare!
And all who travel the narrow way…
Have an inheritance there.

Friend, "Shall We Gather at the River,"
"Just Inside the Eastern Gate"?
We'll sing praises to God forever,
There where Christian loved ones wait…
In that "Land Fairer Than Day."

"An inheritance incorruptible, and undefiled,
and that fadeth not away, reserved in heaven for you,
Who are kept by the power of God through faith
unto salvation ready to be revealed in the last time."
(1Pet 1:4-5)

Wonderful Words!

"Wonderful Words of Life"
Are found in God's Holy Word,
Words that tell of Jesus Christ…
Greatest story ever heard!

"Holy Bible, Book Divine,"
Words of love, forgiveness, grace,
Feed my spirit, soul, and mind,
Till I see my Savior's face…
Such "Wonderful Words of Life"!

Jesus said: "It is written, Man shall not live by
bread alone, but by every word that proceedeth
out of the mouth of God."
(Matt 4:4)

Send Me

Christian, "Serve the Lord with Gladness,"
His gospel message send;
"Let Others See Jesus in You,"
His Spirit dwells within.

"Lord, Lay Some Soul upon My Heart"
And draw that soul to Thee,
"Make Me a Channel of Blessing,"
Here am I, Lord, "Send Me."

"I heard the voice of the Lord, saying,
Whom shall I send, and who will go for us?
Then said I, Here am I; send me."
(Isa 6:8)

Lord, Lead Me On

"Lord, Lead Me On" to "Higher Ground,"
Make me Holy and pure;
Evil forces are all around…
Yet in Thee, I'm secure.

O "Take My Life and Let It Be"
A witness every day;
Thou hast "Redeemed" and set me free….
"Lord, Lead Me On," I pray.

"For thou art my rock and my fortress;
therefore for thy name's sake
lead me, and guide me."
(Ps 31:3)

I Must Tell Jesus

When my hopes and dreams fall apart,
I know just what to do;
"I Must Tell Jesus" my troubles...
He always sees me through.

And those times when I feel cast down,
I cannot stay there long;
For "Jesus, Lover of my Soul,"
Fills my heart with a song!

"The LORD will command his lovingkindness
in the day-time, and in the night his song
shall be with me, and my prayer
unto the God of my life."
(Ps 42:8)

Close to Thee

Lord, keep me "Close to Thee," I pray,
"I Need Thee Every Hour."
For as I walk the pilgrim way,
I'm lost without Thy power.

Just like a ship without a sail,
I'd drift on life's stormy sea,
But, anchored in Thee, I'll not fail...
If I'll just walk "Close to Thee."

"He giveth power to the faint, and to them
that have no might he increaseth strength."
(Isa 40:29)

Just Trust Him!

Friend, God is not dead, He's alive!
He's with you every day.
Oh, "Give Your Best to the Master,"
Walk in His righteous way.

And when those troubles and trials come,
Just rest them in His hand;
"Faith is the Victory," my friend,
He has a perfect plan...
Just trust Him!

"Trust in the LORD with all thine heart;
and lean not unto thine own understanding."
(Pro 3:5)

O The Love of God!

"The Love of God" is love indeed!
Forgiving, endless, and true.
He sent His Son, His Holy Seed,
To save and make us new.

O Lord, my God, "I Stand Amazed"
That you would love us so.
"We Lift Our Hearts in Songs of Praise,"
Such sweet peace You bestow!
O "The Love of God"!

"In this was manifested the love of God toward us,
because that God sent his only begotten Son
into the world, that we might live through him."
(1Jn 4:9)

In The Presence of Jehovah

"In The Presence of Jehovah,"
Let's lift our voice in praise...
As we sense His "Sweet, Sweet Spirit,"
Our hearts to Him are raised.

Worldly pleasures lose their glitter
In the light of our King;
O come, let's serve Him together,
As we rejoice and sing...
"In The Presence of Jehovah."

"Serve the LORD with gladness:
come before his presence with singing."
(Ps 100:2)

Keep Me True, Lord

"Keep Me True, Lord Jesus, keep me true."
"Be Thou My Vision" each day.
"Draw Me Nearer" than ever to You...
As I walk the narrow way.

"Thy Word Have I Hid In My Heart,"
So that I may follow You;
I pray I would never depart...
O Lord my God, "Keep Me True."

"Let us draw near with a true heart in full
assurance of faith, having our hearts sprinkled
from an evil conscience, and our bodies
washed with pure water."
(Heb 10:22)

He Cares for You!

"O How I Love Jesus," my Lord!
His pure blood set me free.
His Holy Spirit dwells within,
Leading and guiding me.

There's no other friend like Him,
"No, Not One" anywhere.
"'Tis So Sweet to Trust in Jesus,"
And to rest in His care...
And He cares for you!

"Casting all your care upon him;
for he careth for you."
(1Pet 5:7)

That Old Time Religion

"'Tis The Old Time Religion"
That reaches deep in the soul,
Revealing the truth of God...
Making the lost sinner whole.

O "How Firm a Foundation,"
Resting on "The Solid Rock,"
Praising God for salvation,
Having heard the Spirit knock...
"Give me That Old Time Religion."

"For I am the LORD, I change not."
"Jesus Christ the same yesterday,
and to-day, and for ever."
(Mal 3:6a; Heb 13:8)

Do You Know Him?

Friend, "Do You Know Him Today?"
Is Christ the LORD your King?
Have your sins been washed away?
Have you a song to sing?

"When the Home Gates Swing Open,"
And Jesus comes again,
Will He say, "Well Done, My Child,"
And take you by the hand?
Do You Know Him?

"And hereby we do know that we know him,
if we keep his commandments."
(1Jn 2:3)

God Leads Us

Over the steepest mountains,
And through the darkest vale,
"Living for Jesus" each day...
Friend, we can never fail.

"God Leads Us Along" life's path;
He shows the way to go,
And as we follow our Lord...
The path takes on a glow.

"Thy word is a lamp unto my feet,
and a light unto my path."
(Ps 119:105)

Walking in Sunlight

"Walking in Sunlight" with Jesus,
When the day is dark and grim,
"O Happy Day" whatever comes,
When we stay focused on Him.

Friend, "Jesus is Lord of All,"
And whatever takes place around,
"Heavenly Sunlight" fills our souls...
"We Have Heard the Joyful Sound."

"Blessed is the people that know
the joyful sound: they shall walk,
O Lord, in the light of Thy countenance."
(Ps 89:15)

No Other Name

"The Church's One Foundation"
Is Jesus Christ, God's Son.
He alone can give salvation;
In Him, the battle's won.

He's "The Solid Rock" of ages,
Forevermore the same,
And our only hope of Glory...
There is "No Other Name."

"Neither is there salvation in any other;
for there is none other name under heaven
given among men, whereby we must be saved."
(Acts 4:12)

Hallelujah Side

O what wonderful fellowship,
When in our Lord we abide!
We're living in His great Kingdom...
On the "Hallelujah Side."

There's not a demon anywhere
That can drag our spirit down;
We're "Safe in the Arms of Jesus,"
His presence is all around...
On the "Hallelujah Side."

"Glory and honour are in his presence;
strength and gladness are in his place."
(1Ch 16:27)

Send a Revival

Our nation is on sinking sand,
We need to bend our knee.
O Lord God, "Revive Us Again"...
Turn our hearts back to Thee.

"Living for Jesus" we are free,
And our nation is blessed,
But we have drifted far away
And reaped a life of stress...
O "Lord, Send a Revival."

"Wilt thou not revive us again:
that thy people may rejoice in thee?"
(Ps 85:6)

Lovely, Lovely Name

There are so many beautiful names,
But one thing is for sure...
"Jesus is the Sweetest Name I Know,"
It is Holy and pure.

"It's a Lovely, Lovely Name," my friend,
A Name revered and praised!
And He's just as precious as His Name...
Full of mercy and grace.

"At the name of Jesus every knee should bow,
of things in heaven, and things in earth,
and things under the earth."
(Phil 2:10)

Come, Ye Thankful People

"Come, Ye Thankful People, Come,"
Let's spread God's Word around.
Tell how He sent forth His Son
That the lost may be found.

O "Send the Light" far and near,
Reaching out every day...
Nothing is more important
Than showing a soul the way.

Jesus said: "Let your light so shine before men,
that they may see your good works,
and glorify your Father which is in heaven."
(Matt 5:16)

There's Power in the Blood

There's "Power in the Blood" of the Lamb...
Power to redeem from sin.
When forgiven by the great I Am,
O what peace and joy within!

Thank God for the precious blood
Shed on "The Old Rugged Cross."
Had it not been for the blood of Christ,
We'd still be empty and lost.
There's "Power in the Blood"!

"Forasmuch as ye know that ye were not redeemed
with corruptible things, as silver and gold, from
your vain conversation received by tradition from
your fathers; But with the precious blood of Christ,
as of a lamb without blemish and without spot."
(1Pet 1:18-19)

Onward Christian Soldiers!

March "Onward Christian Soldiers,"
Till we reach "Higher Ground."
"Stand Up, Stand Up for Jesus,"
He'll never let you down.

As a "Soldier of the Cross,"
March on to victory...
Friend, "It Will Be Worth It All"
When our Lord's face we see...
"Onward Christian Soldiers!"

"Thou therefore endure hardness, as a
good soldier of Jesus Christ."
(2Tim 2:3)

When We Walk with the Lord

My friend, "When We Walk with the Lord,"
He blesses us every day;
And "Standing On the Promises,"
He so gently leads the way.

It matters not how deep the vale,
Nor how fierce the storm may be,
We're "Safe in the Arms of Jesus,"
Throughout all eternity...
"When We Walk with the Lord."

"As ye therefore have received Christ Jesus
the Lord, so walk ye in him."
(Col 2:6)

166

Tell Me the Story of Jesus

"Tell Me the Story of Jesus"
Over and over again,
For I never tire of hearing
Of the loving Savior's hand.

Tell how the hand that made the world
Was nailed to a rugged tree,
And, tell how "Jesus Paid it All,"
Because He loves you and me...
"Tell Me the Story of Jesus."

"He gave himself for our sins, that he might
deliver us from this present evil world,
according to the will of God and our Father;
To whom be glory for ever and ever. Amen."
(Gal 1:4-5)

Walking Through the Storms

Christian, when we walk through the storms
We need not ever fear;
We're "Sheltered in the Arms of God"
Till all is bright and clear.

Praise Him "Till the Storm Passes By,"
Give Him glory each day;
He's working all things for our good,
As we walk in His way.

"And we know that all things work together
for good to them that love God, to them
who are the called according to his purpose."
(Rom 8:28)

The Very Thought of Thee!

"Jesus, the Very Thought of Thee"
Rejoices my heart and soul.
O what "Wonderful Peace" is mine
Since, by grace, You made me whole.

Thy marvelous "Love Lifted Me"
From the depths of sinking sand,
Planting me on "The Solid Rock,"
Where I shall forever stand...
O "The Very thought of Thee"!

"He only is my rock and my salvation:
he is my defence; I shall not be moved."
(Ps 62:6)

Such a Precious Name!

"All Hail the Power of Jesus Name,"
"Precious Name, O how sweet!"
He's King of kings, and Lord of lords,
Let's worship at His feet!

At His Name "Every Knee Shall Bow,"
For some…"Too Late to Pray."
We must come to the Savior now
And walk His righteous way…
Jesus, such a "Precious Name"!

"Wherefore God also hath highly exalted him,
and given him a name which is above every name."
(Phil 2:9)

What a Savior!

Our Savior was with the Father
When all the worlds were made;
Then He came...born of a virgin,
Our sinful souls to save...
"Hallelujah! What a Savior!"

Persecution, tribulation,
So much today we see;
Yet still "He's Pouring Out Blessings"
On souls who've been set free...
"Hallelujah! What a Savior!"

"And all these blessings shall come on thee,
and overtake thee, if thou shalt harken unto
the voice of the Lord thy God."
(Deut 28:2)

Let Us Sing Praises!

"All Creatures of Our God and King"
Sing praises to His Name!
"Lift Up, Lift Up Your Voices Now,"
His message to proclaim.

"O For a Thousand Tongues to Sing"
"To God Be the Glory,"
Lifting "The Banner of the Cross,"
Sharing His love story...
Let Us Sing Praises!

"Sing praises to God, sing praises: sing praises
unto our King, sing praises."
(Ps 47:6)

He Builds His Church!

Built upon Christ, "The Solid Rock,"
The Rock of our salvation,
"'Tis a Glorious Church," my friend,
O "How Firm a Foundation"!

The gates of hell shall not prevail
Against the church our Lord builds;
For the Son of the Living God
Purifies, strengthens, and fills...
As He Builds His Church!

"He (Jesus) saith unto them, But whom do
ye say that I am?" "Peter answered and said,
Thou art the Christ, the son of the living God."
Jesus said: "Upon this rock I will build my church;
And the gates of hell shall not prevail against it."
(Matt 16:15, 16, 18b)

Wonderful Grace!

The "Wonderful Grace of Jesus,"
By which sinners are saved,
Is "Amazing Grace" that frees us...
Our sin debt's fully paid!

Praise God, "Grace, Greater Than Our Sin,"
Reaches the vilest soul;
And the cleansing blood of Jesus
Purifies and makes whole...
O such "Wonderful Grace"!

"For by grace are ye saved through faith;
and that not of yourselves: it is the gift of God."
(Eph 2:8)

Give Me Jesus!

I can do without so many things
As I walk the pilgrim path,
But "Without Him" I would surely sink...
Into a sea of wrath.

O friend, "Mine Eyes Have Seen the Glory,"
"He's Everything to me."
"Take This Whole World, but Give me Jesus,"
He fills my heart with glee!

"The LORD is my rock, and my fortress, and my
deliverer; my God, my strength, in whom
I will trust; my buckler, and the horn of
my salvation, and my high tower."
(Ps 18:2)

We've a Story to Tell

Christian, "We've a Story to Tell"
That can set the captive free...
Let's "Go tell it on the Mountain"
And to everyone we see.

Tell how sin can be forgiven,
Thanks to "The Old Rugged Cross,"
How Christ left His Home in Heaven,
To give new life to the lost...
"We've a Story to Tell!"

Jesus said: "Go ye into all the world, and preach the
gospel to every creature."
(Mk 16:15)

Light of the World

"The Light of the World is Jesus."
"Without Him" all is so grim!
"The Sands of Time are Sinking," friend;
Let your Light shine bright for Him.

O how "People Need the Lord"
To redeem and guide them through!
"Set My Soul Afire," Lord Jesus...
Make me a witness for You.

"For thou shalt be his witness unto all men
of what thou hast seen and heard."
(Acts 22:15)

Our Hiding Place

In "The Family of God," we're safe!
Our souls are hidden in Christ;
There is no safer hiding place
Than in Him who is our life.

We're "Sheltered in the Arms of God."
What have we ever to fear?
"Rejoice, Rejoice, ye Christians,"
His Holy Spirit is here...
He's our hiding place.

"He that dwelleth in the secret place
of the most High shall abide under the
shadow of the Almighty."
(Ps 91:1)

As I Bow

O "Spirit of the Living God,"
I bow before Thee meekly;
Take all that I am, heart and soul...
"Fill My Cup, Lord," completely!

"Search Me, O God," reveal to me
Those sins I have failed to see;
O "Just a Closer Walk with Thee,
Grant it, Jesus, is my plea"...
As I bow on bended knee.

"O come, let us worship and bow down:
let us kneel before the LORD our maker."
(Ps 95:6)

A Song in the Air

Friend, "There's A Song in the Air,"
A joyful melody;
Open your heart and you'll hear
A gorgeous harmony.

O such a "Sweet Hour of Prayer"!
Our hearts rejoice and sing....
Yes, "There's A Song In the Air"
When we worship our King.

"Speaking to yourselves in psalms and hymns
and spiritual songs, singing and making
melody in your heart to the Lord."
(Eph 5:19)

A Little Talk With Jesus

When troubles have gotten you down,
And you feel you can't go on,
"Just Have A Little Talk With Jesus"
On "The Royal Telephone."

He will lift you to "Higher Ground,"
You'll hear Him "Whispering Hope"…
"God Will Take Care of You," my friend;
He'll give you the strength to cope.
"Just Have A Little Talk With Jesus."

"He shall call upon me, and I will answer him:
I will be with him in trouble; I will deliver him,
and honour him."
(Ps 91:15)

Honey in the Rock

On Jesus Christ, "The Solid Rock,"
The Christian's life is built.
Praise God, as we bow before Him...
He removes sin and guilt.

O come to "The Rock of Ages"...
Come and be made whole.
"There's Honey in the Rock," my friend,
To satisfy your soul.

"For he satisfieth the longing soul,
and filleth the hungry soul with goodness."
(Ps 107:9)

O Precious Fountain!

"There Is a Fountain Filled with blood"
That washes the vilest soul…
And all who come to this fountain
Can be made perfectly whole.

His blood was poured out for you, friend,
Surrender your all to Christ…
You'll be "Constantly Abiding"
With Him in eternal life…
O Precious Fountain!

"For with thee is the fountain of life,
in thy light shall we see light."
(Ps 36:9)

Forever Free!

"One Day," "I'll Fly Away"...
To that "Meeting in the Air."
"Glory, Glory, Hallelujah,"
What a grand reunion there!

Friend, "When We All Get to Heaven,"
O "What a Day That Will Be"!
Such rejoicing will fill our souls...
"Home At Last," forever free!

"For the Lord himself shall descend
from heaven with a shout, with the voice
of the archangel, and with the trump of God:
and the dead in Christ shall rise first:
Then we which are alive and remain shall be
caught up together with them in the air:
and so shall we ever be with the Lord."
(1Thes 4:16-17)

The Wondrous Cross

"Alas, and Did My Savior Bleed,"
There on that old rugged tree...
"Such Love," such "Amazing Love,"
He gave all to set us free.

"When I Survey the Wondrous Cross,"
I cannot help but bow down...
My heart is filled with joyful praise,
I was lost, but now I'm found...
Thanks to the wondrous cross.

"The preaching of the cross is to them that perish
foolishness; but unto us which are saved
it is the power of God."
(1Cor 1:18)

Moment By Moment

Lord Jesus, "Moment By Moment,"
"My Faith Looks Up to Thee,"
And whatever troubles may come,
You're there to comfort me.

"All That Thrills My Soul" is You, Lord,
"Draw me Nearer," I pray;
Take all I am or hope to be,
Lead me Thy Holy way...
"Moment By Moment."

"For thou art my rock and my fortress;
therefore for thy name's sake
lead me, and guide me."
(Ps 31:3)

The Haven of Rest

Whenever I'm tired and weary,
With burdens so hard to bear,
I flee to "The Haven of Rest"
And my load is lifted there.

"Sweet Peace, the Gift of God's Love,"
Is found in that holy place;
"Where Could I Go But to the Lord"
To receive mercy and grace?
He's "The Haven of Rest."

Jesus said: "Come unto me, all ye that labour
and are heavy laden, and I will give you rest."
(Matt 11:28)

He Leadeth Me

"Every Day with Jesus," my Lord,
I find such joy and peace.
"He Leadeth Me, O Blessed Thought!"
In Him my soul doth feast.

"The Love of God" is all around,
It's just so plain to see;
"Where He Leads Me I Will Follow"…
"He's Everything to Me!"

Jesus said: "My sheep hear my voice,
and I know them, and they follow me."
(Jn 10:27)

Be a Light For Jesus

Christian, "Be a Light For Jesus"
As you walk in His way;
Call the lost to our loving Lord,
Before the Judgment Day.

O "Send the Light" into darkness,
Where souls are steeped in sin;
He came not to call the righteous,
But lost sinners to win.

Jesus said: "I came not to call the righteous,
but sinners to repentance."
(Lk 5:32)

We Can Know

"I Know Whom I Have Believed,"
And "It Is Well With My Soul."
"'Tis So Sweet To Trust In Jesus,"
The great Shepherd of the fold.

Such "Blessed Assurance" is mine
"Since Jesus Came Into My Heart."
O "The Glory of His Presence"
When His Spirit He imparts!

"Hereby we know that he abideth
in us, by the Spirit he hath given us."
(1Jn 3:24b)

Name Above All Names

"Take the Name of Jesus With You,"
As you walk the pilgrim way;
That precious "Name Above All Names"
Will brighten the darkest day.

Lift high "The Banner of the Cross,"
Proclaim His Word as you go;
"Let Others See Jesus In You,"
As His love through you doth flow.

"Wherefore God also hath highly exalted him,
and given him a name which is above every name."
(Phil 2:9)

Worship His Majesty

"What a Fellowship" is ours in Christ!
Such wonderful joy divine!
He came to give abundant life...
In Him great treasures we find!

"What a Friend We Have in Jesus!"
"He Is So Precious to Me."
And "He Is Worthy" to be praised...
O "Worship His Majesty"!

"Bless the LORD, O my soul. O LORD my God,
thou art very great; thou art clothed with
honour and majesty."
(Ps 104:1)

His Eye Is On the Sparrow

God knows each thing we say and do.
He misses nothing at all;
For "His Eye Is On the Sparrow"...
He takes note if it should fall.

He taught that little bird to sing
And fly high into the tree...
We, too, are taught by our great King...
"The Song of a Soul Set Free!"

"If the Son therefore shall make you free,
ye shall be free indeed."
(Jn 8:36)

The Light of Christ

The Light of Christ, our Lord who came,
Burns bright within the soul
Of all who bear His "Precious Name,"
Forgiven and made whole.

O Lord God, "Set My Soul Afire,"
With Your Light from above;
"Make Me a Channel of Blessing,"
Shining the Light of Your love.

"The love of God is shed abroad in our hearts
by the Holy Ghost which is given unto us."
(Rom 5:5b)

Surrender All

Lord, "I Surrender All" to Thee...
All I have and all I am.
"Take My Life and Let It Be"
Thine alone, O Holy Lamb.

Friend, surrender your all to Christ;
"Let Him Have His Way With Thee."
He will pour out blessings on you...
And set your spirit free.

"Being then made free from sin,
ye became the servants of righteousness."
(Rom 6:18)

This World Is Not My Home

"I Can't feel at Home in This World,"
No matter where I roam;
I'm just a pilgrim passing through...
"This World Is Not My Home."

"I Am Bound for the Promised Land,"
"Down By the Riverside,"
Soon I'll enter "The Eastern Gate"...
Forever to abide.

"It is written, Eye hath not seen, nor ear heard,
neither have entered into the heart of man,
the things which God hath prepared for
them that love him."
(1Cor 2:9)

Trusting Jesus

"How Marvelous" to trust the Lord!
He's worthy of all praise.
Oh, "The Glory of His Presence"…
When we walk in His ways.

"Constantly Abiding" in Him,
We have a song to sing;
For His grace is all sufficient!
We can face anything…
"Trusting Jesus."

"They that trust in the LORD shall be as
mount Zion, which cannot be removed,
but abideth for ever."
(Ps 125:1)

He Gives a Song

"There is Sunshine in My Soul Today,"
Even the dark clouds look bright!
"Since Jesus Came into My Heart,"
My soul is filled with His Light.

O "I Just Can't Praise Him Enough,"
"He Touched Me, and Made Me Whole."
"Blessed Be the Name of the Lord,"
He gives a song to the soul!

"Sing unto the LORD, O ye saints of his,
and give thanks at the remembrance of his holiness."
(Ps 30:4)

I Love You, Lord!

"O God, Our Help in Ages Past,"
"I Need Thee Every Hour."
"Give Me That Old Time Religion,"
Thy Spirit, and Thy Power.

I love "The B-I-B-L-E,"
"Holy Bible, Book Divine,"
And I love old hymns of the faith,
What precious treasures are mine!
"I Love You, Lord!"

Jesus said: "Where your treasure is,
there will your heart be also."
(Matt 6:21)

No Other Foundation

On "The Old Rugged Cross," my friend,
We see love beyond compare!
"Burdens Are Lifted At Calvary,"
As we surrender all there.

"This is the Day the Lord Hath Made,"
Day allowed for salvation!
O come to the "Rock of Ages,"
There's no other foundation!

"For other foundation can no man lay
than that is laid, which is Jesus Christ."
(1Cor 3:11)

Something About That Name

How I love the Name of Jesus!
"There's Something About That Name."
No other name on earth frees us...
O thank God our Savior came!

Yes, friend, "His Name Is Wonderful,"
For He's our Glorious King!
Let us give "Glory to His Name,"
As our hearts rejoice and sing...
"There's Something About That Name."

"O LORD our Lord, how excellent is thy name
in all the earth!"
(Ps 8:9)

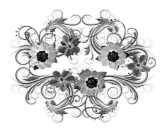

One Day At a Time

"One Day At a Time," Lord Jesus,
We know we can make it through;
No storm will ever come our way
That's more powerful than You.

If we'll simply "Trust and Obey"
When we do not understand,
We're sure to find "Wonderful Peace,"
Trusting in You and Your plan...
"One Day At a Time."

"Trust in the LORD with all thine heart;
and lean not unto thine own understanding.
In all thy ways acknowledge him, and he
shall direct thy paths."
(Pro 3:5-6)

What a Day That Will Be!

O "Blessed Day of Rest and Cheer"
When our Lord's face we see;
No more pain, suffering, or fear...
We'll be completely free!

"Just Over In the Glory Land,"
Where Christian loved ones wait,
We'll sing these Hymns with Gabriel's band...
"Inside the Eastern Gate."
"What a Day That Will Be!"

"Let the word of Christ dwell in you richly
in all wisdom; teaching and admonishing
one another in psalms and hymns and
spiritual song, singing with grace in your
hearts to the Lord."
(Col 3:16)

Index of Poems

Index of Poems

Index of Poems